ASTRONAUT ACADEMY

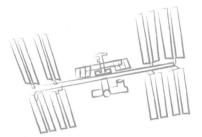

First American Edition 2016
Kane Miller, A Division of EDC Publishing

Copyright © 2016 Ivy Kids (an imprint of Ivy Press Ltd)

For information contact:
Kane Miller, A Division of EDC Publishing
PO Box 470663
Tulsa, OK 74147-0663
www.kanemiller.com
www.edcpub.com
www.usbornebooksandmore.com

Library of Congress Control Number: 2015954191

Printed in China

ISBN: 978-1-61067-470-6

10 9 8 7 6 5 4 3

ASTRONAUT ACADEMY

WRITTEN BY
STEVE MARTIN

ILLUSTRATED BY
JENNIFER FARLEY

Kane Miller
A DIVISION OF EDC PUBLISHING

CONTENTS

SPACE SCIENTIST

SPACE GYM

SPACE EXPLORER

SPACE GOODIES!

WELCOME TO ASTRONAUT ACADEMY!

Congratulations on choosing the most exciting job on (and off) the planet. You have decided to join a brave group of men and women who are willing to leave the safety of Earth and travel into the depths of space. Do you have what it takes to be an astronaut? Your training starts here.

Astronauts don't just float around in space having fun. You need to be an explorer, a pilot, a scientist, an engineer and a repair worker. During your time at the Astronaut Academy, you will attend different classes. Each lesson will test your physical and mental abilities.

Humans have already landed on the Moon and the next challenge is Mars. Astronauts will travel for many months across the vastness of space to reach this amazing, mysterious planet.

And this is the mission you are going to train for because you're going with them!

Imagine being the first person to ever set foot on another planet . . .

So, fill in your ID card, turn the page and begin your training.

GOOD LUCK, SPACE CADET!

During your training, you will earn certificates for different astronaut roles.

Before you start, please register at the Astronaut Academy. Fill in your details on the Space Cadet ID Card.

MARS

EARTH

SPACE CADET ID

FIRST NAME:

LAST NAME:

AGE:

NATIONALITY:

DATE JOINED:

MEET THE CREW

At the Academy, you will train for every role on the spacecraft, from pilot to scientist. This makes you more likely to be chosen for a mission and allows you to take over if one of your crew members becomes ill. It also prepares you for one-person missions.

To qualify in each astronaut role and graduate from the Astronaut Academy you must complete the tasks in this book and earn all your certificates. Only then will you be ready for a mission to Mars . . .

ASTRONAUT PILOTS

command and fly the spacecraft during missions. They need to know how to control the spacecraft during liftoff, how to fly in space, how to link up with a space station and how to land safely back on Earth.

MISSION SPECIALISTS

are engineers and scientists. They carry out experiments in space, operate specialized equipment, go on space walks and are prepared to fix anything from the tiniest devices to enormous spacecraft parts.

PAYLOAD SPECIALISTS

are not full-time astronauts. They are experts in their own areas and join missions to help with particular scientific experiments or technical tasks. Just like other astronauts, they need to be fit in order to live and work in space.

SPACE INFO

—QUICK— THINKING:

IMPROVING YOUR REACTION TIMES

Astronaut pilots need to respond quickly in lots of different situations, from landing a spacecraft to carrying out repairs in space and dealing with emergencies.

In the 1950s, the first astronauts were chosen from military jet pilots because they were able to think and react super fast. Today, astronauts come from many different backgrounds and include teachers, scientists and engineers.

TEST AND IMPROVE YOUR REACTION TIMES

You will need: a 12-inch ruler

1. Ask a friend to hold the top of the ruler with his or her thumb and finger.

2. Stand opposite and place one hand at the bottom of the ruler, so your thumb and finger line up with the zero mark, but are not touching it. Your thumb and fingers should be approximately 1 inch away from the ruler.

3. Ask your friend to let go of the ruler without any warning, so that it drops between your thumb and finger. Catch it as quickly as possible, and record your measurement below. Repeat six times.

4. Keep practicing over three days. Start with your strongest hand (the hand you write with) and then try with your other hand for an extra challenge.

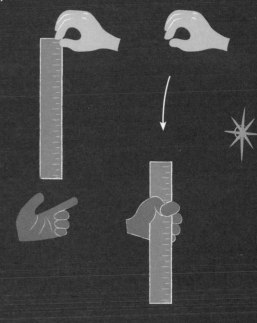

In the boxes below, record the measurement where you caught the ruler. The smaller the measurement, the faster your reaction time.

You should find that your reaction time gets faster and faster each day.

ATTEMPT	1	2	3	4	5	6
DAY 1						
DAY 2						
DAY 3						

Place your Mission Complete sticker here when you have completed your reaction training.

PLACE STICKER HERE

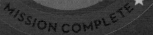

★ MISSION COMPLETE ★

T-MINUS . . . GETTING READY FOR BLASTOFF!

10 - 9 - 8 - 7 - 6 - 5 - 4 - 3 - 2 - 1

Everyone who has ever watched a space movie has heard the ten seconds to blastoff countdown. But the real countdown begins long before ten seconds.

NASA, which stands for the National Aeronautics and Space Administration, is the US government's space organization. NASA uses the expression "T-minus" for its countdowns: T (for "time") is the moment the spacecraft blasts off, so T-minus 30 minutes would mean 30 minutes before blastoff.

T-MINUS . . .

43 HOURS
* Countdown clock starts
* Flight deck inspected
* Navigation system tested

27 HOURS
* Launch area cleared of nonessential people

19 HOURS
* Crew module cleaned
* Engines prepared for fueling

11 HOURS
* Weather briefing takes place
* Final crew equipment loaded

6 HOURS
* Fuel tank filled

2 MINUTES
* Astronauts close and lock visors

3 HOURS
* Final shuttle inspection takes place
* Astronauts enter shuttle
* Crew hatch closed

7 SECONDS
* Main engine started

20 MINUTES
* Onboard computers set to launch

0 SECONDS
* Boosters ignited, causing fuel to burn and the spacecraft to . . .

9 MINUTES
* Flight recorders activated
* Automatic launch sequence started

BLAST OFF!

5 MINUTES
* Support systems power unit started

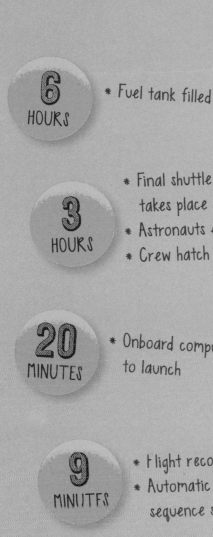

i
SPACE INFO

FLYING AND LANDING THE SPACE SHUTTLE

NASA's space shuttles are probably the most well-known of all spacecraft. From 1981 to 2011, they were used to take astronauts into space. Fast and able to carry huge cargoes, they were perfect for building the International Space Station, which was put together in space, piece by piece.

The shuttle needed a massive amount of power for liftoff. It had to carry almost **440,000 gallons** of liquid oxygen and liquid hydrogen, which were mixed and burned to power the engines. 440,000 gallons is almost enough liquid to fill an Olympic-size swimming pool!

The shuttle flew directly upward for 40 seconds, then flipped onto its back and continued to go up for another five minutes. It then turned right-side up and, less than nine minutes after takeoff, it was in orbit.

Traveling around and around the Earth is known as being in orbit. To do this, the shuttle reached a speed of about **17,400 mph**—more than 30 times faster than a jet airplane!

When coming in to land back on Earth, the pilot switched off the engines and the shuttle glided to the runway. Landing was difficult because the shuttle approached the runway at an angle of 20 degrees. This is about seven times steeper than an airplane landing!

When it was **2,000 feet** from the ground, the nose was pulled up to slow the shuttle down to **290 mph**. The landing wheels were then lowered and a parachute opened to help the shuttle stop.

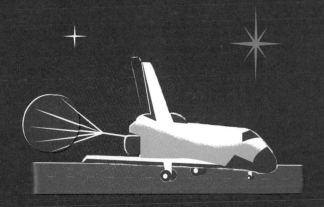

NOW IT'S TIME TO FLY YOUR VERY OWN SPACECRAFT!
On the cover flaps of this book, there is a model of a spacecraft that you can cut out and slot together.

To make your model:

1. Cut out the pieces along the solid lines.

2. Nose: Shape into a cone and glue tab 1 to 1. To attach the Nose to the Body, glue tab 2 to 2 on the Body, tab 3 to 3 and so on.

3. Body: Roll the body piece into a tube and glue tab 6 to 6.

4. Point: Fold the Point along the dotted line and glue tab 7 to 7. To attach the Point to the Nose, glue tab 8 to 8 on the outside of the Nose and tab 9 to 9.

5. Boosters: Fold each Booster along the dotted lines. Glue tabs 10 and 11 to 10 and 11 on the Body, tabs 12 and 13 to 12 and 13 on the Body and so on.

Once you have built your spacecraft, place your Mission Complete sticker here.

PLACE STICKER HERE

★ MISSION COMPLETE ★

DOCKING YOUR SPACESHIP

When a spacecraft connects to another spacecraft or space station it is called docking. Docking means that astronauts can move from one vehicle to the other. Every astronaut pilot must be able to do this.

Since the year 2000, astronaut crews have been living on the International Space Station. The astronauts are taken to the Space Station by spacecraft.

Every trip involves a docking procedure, which is very tricky because:

* The Space Station is traveling at 5 miles every second.
* It is not traveling in a straight line because it is circling Earth.
* The station weighs about **463 tons,** which is more than 320 cars!
* The docking spacecraft must also travel at 5 miles per second and may weigh over 110 tons.
* The pilot has to be accurate to within **3 inches** for the docking to work!

And if all that doesn't make it hard enough, the pilot has to approach the docking station backward!

HOW TO DOCK

The spacecraft must first move into the same orbit as the space station. The pilot turns the spacecraft so that its hatch faces the space station's docking station. When the spacecraft is lined up with the dock, the pilot moves it carefully onto the docking ring, where it is fitted into place.

The passageway between the spacecraft and the space station is slowly filled with air so the crew can move into the space station.

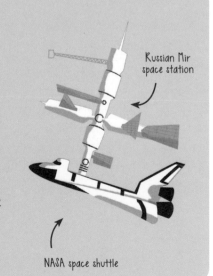

Russian Mir space station

NASA space shuttle

SPACE DOCK CHALLENGE

PRACTICE YOUR DOCKING SKILLS

You will need:

a piece of string   a rubber band   two plastic cups   a blindfold   a friend

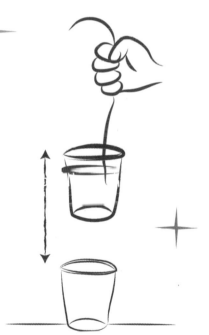

1. Put the rubber band around one cup, near the top.

2. Tie the string around the rubber band.

3. The cup should be held about 6 inches from the floor. This is the docking spacecraft.

4. Blindfold your friend.

5. Place the second cup on the floor. This is the docking station.

6. Steer your friend toward the docking station using instructions such as "Forward two paces," "Left 2 inches."

7. When your friend is holding the cup above the docking station, use the command "Dock!"

8. If your friend docks without knocking over the docking station, you have successfully completed the task.

When you have successfully docked, place your Mission Complete sticker here. →

PLACE STICKER HERE

MISSION COMPLETE

MISSION CONTROL

Mission Control in Houston, TX, provides vital support to all NASA space flights and their crew and pilots. It is staffed by highly skilled scientists, engineers and technicians every hour of every day throughout the year.

There may be up to **20 CONSOLES** (control panels) in a Control Room, each staffed by an officer with a specific job. One might monitor communications systems, another might check the onboard computers and a third might maintain the navigation systems.

There is always a **SURGEON CONSOLE** at Mission Control. This is staffed by a doctor who is a specialist in caring for astronauts in space.

The Control Room that was used for all of the Apollo space missions—including Apollo 11, the first moon landing in 1969—has been kept as a museum.

Each spacecraft has its own Control Room and team. For example, the experts looking after the Space Station are based in the International Space Station Flight Control Room.

FLIGHT CONTROLLERS keep an eye on the spacecraft's systems to make sure everything is going according to plan.

ENGINEERS AND TECHNICIANS learn how to support space missions in the Training Flight Control Room. They also use this to practice dealing with emergencies.

FLIGHT DIRECTOR leads the Mission Control Team. It is his or her job to make sure the mission is successful.

FLIGHT DIRECTOR

i

SPACE INFO

DRESSING FOR WORK

What do your parents wear for work? A suit? A uniform? For an astronaut, dressing for work is different and much more complicated. It takes more than an hour to put on a space suit, and that's with people helping!

HELMET: protects the head, holds oxygen, has cameras and lights

SNOOPY CAP: has earphones and a microphone

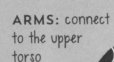

PLSS: the Primary Life Support Subsystem

UPPER TORSO: made out of fiberglass

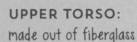

ARMS: connect to the upper torso

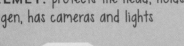

DISPLAYS AND CONTROL MODULE: controls the space suit's operation

TETHER: stops the astronaut from floating away

CUFF CHECKLIST: lists tasks to complete

WRIST MIRROR: to see the control module

EVA GLOVES: contain heaters to keep hands warm

LOWER TORSO: attaches to the upper torso to seal the astronaut into the suit

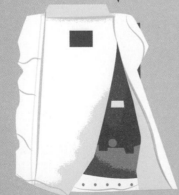

THE SPACE SUIT'S FUNCTIONS INCLUDE:

* Providing oxygen, which is a gas people need to breathe in order to stay alive.

* Allowing the astronaut to work in extreme temperatures.

* Shielding the astronaut from radiation, which is the Sun's energy and is harmful to humans. (On Earth, the atmosphere protects us from these dangerous levels of radiation.)

* Protecting the astronaut from the fast-moving particles that fly around in space. (Spacecraft also need protective armor to prevent damage from these particles.)

* Underneath the space suit, the astronaut wears a liquid cooling garment, through which water flows so the astronaut doesn't become too hot.

Astronauts also wear something called a maximum absorption garment under the space suit. This might sound cool, but it is actually NASA's name for a diaper. You can't visit the bathroom when you're wearing a space suit!

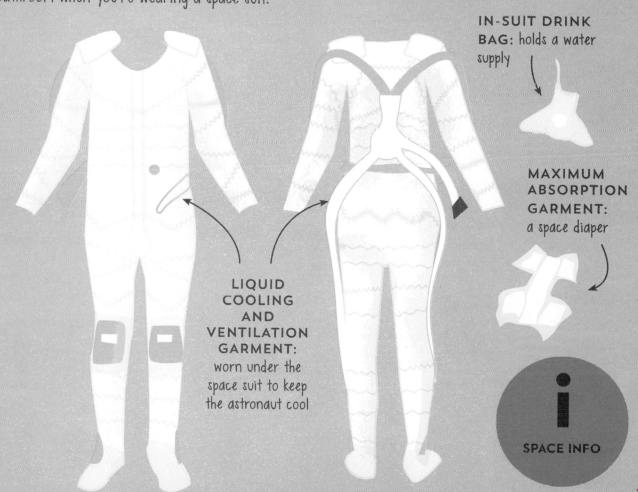

IN-SUIT DRINK BAG: holds a water supply

MAXIMUM ABSORPTION GARMENT: a space diaper

LIQUID COOLING AND VENTILATION GARMENT: worn under the space suit to keep the astronaut cool

i

SPACE INFO

THE INTERNATIONAL SPACE STATION

The International Space Station orbits Earth 16 times a day. It is 358 feet long—almost as long as a football field—and has a solar panel wingspan of 240 feet. It was built in space because it would have been far too large to launch from Earth. More than 115 flights were needed to take all the parts into space to make it. This took 13 years, and cost more than **$98 billion**.

16x

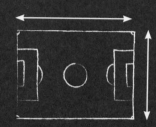

$98,000,000,000

115 flights

The station is used to carry out experiments and test space equipment. It is an international project and visiting astronauts have come from many different countries, including the United States, Canada, Brazil, Russia, Italy, South Korea, Malaysia, Japan and the UK.

Each crew of six astronauts stays aboard for about six months. The station has a living space of 13,700 cubic feet, which is about the same size as **13 living rooms**. Since astronauts are in space with the same people for such a long time, it is important that they get along with each other.

* The station orbits approximately 250 miles above Earth (this is the distance of a five-hour trip by car).

* Two spacecraft are kept permanently docked at the Space Station in case there's an emergency and the crew members need to leave.
* Five space agencies worked together to build the station: NASA (USA), Roscosmos (Russia), the European Space Agency, the Canadian Space Agency and the Japan Aerospace Exploration Agency.

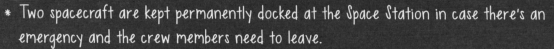

German:
Hallo!

Spanish:
Hola!

French:
Salut!

Russian:
Privet!

Japan:
Konnichiwa!

PRACTICE SAYING "HELLO" IN FIVE LANGUAGES

On the International Space Station, you will be living and working with people from all over the world.

1. Learn how to say "hello!" to your fellow astronauts in their own language.

2. When you have learned the words, ask a friend to test you.

When you've completed this mission, you can add the Mission Complete sticker!

PLACE STICKER HERE

★ MISSION COMPLETE ★

GROW YOUR OWN SPACE FOOD

It will take about six months to fly to Mars. This means that it will be difficult to store all the food the astronauts need for the journey. Ideally, astronauts will grow their own food, which is why they have been doing experiments on the International Space Station to see how plants grow in space.

* Growing your own food in space will be even more important if we build space colonies in the future.

PRACTICE GROWING YOUR OWN FOOD

You will need: cress seeds (you can find these at most garden centers), a small container such as an empty, clean yogurt container, paper towels, cotton balls

1. Take the wrapper off your container.

2. Place the NASA SPACE EXPERIMENT DO NOT TOUCH sticker (from the back of the book) on the container.

3. Scrunch up a sheet of paper towel and wet it. Put the paper towel in the bottom of the container.

* In addition to providing food, plants also improve air quality because they take carbon dioxide from the air and produce oxygen that humans can breathe.

* Astronauts eat a lot of freeze-dried food. This is food that is frozen and has had the water removed from it. It lasts a long time and is easy to store. If you want to try some astronaut food, you can buy freeze-dried fruit at the supermarket.

4. Put some damp cotton balls on top of the paper towel, keeping them below the top of the container.

5. Sprinkle the cress seeds on the cotton balls and press them down.

6. Put the container in a warm place with plenty of light (a windowsill is perfect) and leave the seeds to grow for a few days.

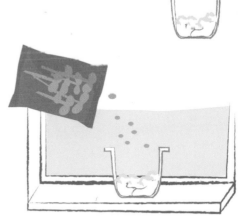

When your seeds have sprouted, place your Mission Complete sticker here. ⟶

PLACE STICKER HERE

★ MISSION COMPLETE ★

FIRST AID — SKILLS —

Since astronauts might be on the International Space Station for months, they must have medicine and first aid equipment—you can't call an ambulance in space! They also need first aid skills.

Medical experts at Mission Control on Earth support the astronauts, and most problems can be dealt with on the Space Station. As a last resort, astronauts can be evacuated to Earth.

If an astronaut sprains their wrist, they will need a sling so they can rest the injured arm.

PRACTICE MAKING A SLING

You will need: a large, square piece of fabric. You might use a pillowcase or a square scarf.

1. Take the square cloth and fold it into a triangle.

2. Ask the injured astronaut to hold their arm in front of their chest with the arm bent at the elbow.

3. Place the sling between the injured arm and the astronaut's body. One point of the triangle should be next to the person's elbow.

4. Tie the top and bottom of the sling together behind the neck. Be careful that it is not too tight at the back. The arm should be pointing up just a little bit.

PLACE STICKER HERE
MISSION COMPLETE

When you have successfully treated the patient, place your Mission Complete sticker here.

Congratulations! You are now a...

QUALIFIED
ASTRONAUT PILOT

NAME: _Bobby_

The above named astronaut
is qualified to be an

ASTRONAUT PILOT
and to take part in the first
manned mission to Mars.

Astronaut Academy would like
to wish you every success in your
historic mission.

GOOD LUCK!

QUALIFICATION DATE: _Today_

SPACE ENGINEER

SPACE FIX!

WORKING IN SPACE WITH GLOVES

Astronauts spend much of their time caring for and repairing equipment. They might be asked to repair anything, from the International Space Station to the Hubble Space Telescope. Tasks often involve working on small, complicated pieces of equipment while wearing thick, heavy space gloves. If that sounds difficult . . . well, it is!

PRACTICE WORKING IN SPACE

This exercise will give you an idea of just how tricky it can be to use your hands for delicate operations while wearing space gloves.

You will need: a pair of thick gloves, such as sports or snow gloves, or two or three pairs of thin gloves

1. Before you begin, put on the gloves.

2. Use a pencil to trace your route through the space maze to Mars in the middle.

MARS

START

When you have made your way through the maze, place your Mission Complete sticker here.

PLACE STICKER HERE

★ MISSION COMPLETE ★

29

SPACE FIX!

HAND-EYE COORDINATION

As an astronaut, you might find yourself outside the spacecraft, fixing equipment in a tricky position while following instructions from Mission Control. You might even have to fix your spacecraft while operating a robotic arm. Being able to coordinate your hand and eye movements is therefore essential.

PRACTICE HAND-EYE COORDINATION

You will need: a pencil and a mirror

1. Follow the line of the spacecraft's trail on the opposite page with a pencil. Easy enough . . . except that you are not allowed to look directly at this page while you are doing it!

2. Stand in front of a mirror and hold the book in front of your chest with one hand so you can see this page in the mirror. Using your other hand, trace the trail with your pencil, making sure you do not go outside the lines.

FINISH!

START

PLACE
STICKER
HERE

★ MISSION COMPLETE ★

When you have successfully traced the route,
place your Mission Complete sticker here.

31

SPACE WALKING

Space walking is an incredible experience because, in the weightlessness of space, **people can actually float**.

It's quite an experience! Imagine floating in the vastness of space, with Earth miles below. The excitement, the beauty of space and the feeling of freedom stay with the space walkers for the rest of their lives.

Although magical, space walks involve a lot of work. Most space walks are performed to carry out repairs to space equipment and an astronaut may spends hours outside on a "walk."

Before venturing out into space, astronauts put on space suits, which protect them, keep them warm and supply oxygen. Next, they enter the space station air lock. This has two doors and stops air from escaping from the station when the astronauts leave. The space walkers go through the first door and close it behind them. Then they open the second door and head off into space.

Astronauts have safety harnesses that keep them from floating off into space. They also wear **jet packs** and can use thrusters to steer their way back to the space station if the harness breaks.

Astronauts refer to space walking as EVA or Extra-Vehicular Activity.

PRACTICE SPACE WALKING!

This will help you practice moving around carefully in the darkness of space.

You will need: six small objects (for example, tennis balls or numbers written on pieces of paper), a flashlight, gloves, rubber boots, a backpack

1. Ask a friend to hide the six objects in a room.

2. Put on the gloves, rubber boots and backpack. Check your space suit with an adult to make sure it is safe before you begin the task.

3. Enter the room and see if you can find all the objects.

4. It might sound easy, but there's a catch . . . the room must be completely dark, although you are allowed to use a flashlight.

When you've found all the objects, your mission is completed and you can collect your sticker. →

PLACE STICKER HERE

★ MISSION COMPLETE ★

UNLUCKY 13:

THE STORY OF APOLLO 13

"Houston, we've had a problem here"

These famous words were uttered by astronaut **Jack Swigert** as Apollo 13's mission to land on the Moon ran into terrible danger 200,000 miles from Earth.

A spark from an exposed wire in one of the spacecraft's oxygen tanks caused an explosion that completely destroyed one tank and damaged another.

The three astronauts on board faced a desperate battle for survival. They needed oxygen to power the fuel cells—without it they couldn't get home. The astronauts, and the technicians at Mission Control, needed to think . . . FAST!

Apollo 13 was actually two spacecraft. The crew members were in
Odyssey, the command module. Odyssey was attached to Aquarius, which was the spacecraft that was to land on the Moon. Luckily, Aquarius hadn't been damaged so it was possible to use it as a space lifeboat

The crew shut down Odyssey's systems to save power (they would still need it to land on Earth). Then, they scrambled through the tunnel connecting it to Aquarius and started up Aquarius' systems. Aquarius was fine for traveling through space, but because it was a Moon lander and didn't have a heat shield, it wouldn't have survived reentry into the Earth's atmosphere.

The crew circled the Moon without landing and turned the spacecraft toward Earth. To save more power, they turned off everything they didn't need on Aquarius and sat in the cold and dark, far, far from home.

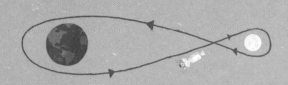

There were no guidance systems on board, so they had to figure out the correct angle for reentry into Earth's atmosphere. If they got it wrong, the spaceship and everything inside it would burn up on reentry.

As they approached Earth, the crew powered up Odyssey for the landing and abandoned Aquarius. Four days after the explosion, the three astronauts safely splashed down into the Pacific Ocean. Their lives had been saved by their ingenuity, teamwork and most importantly, their astronaut training.

SPACE INFO

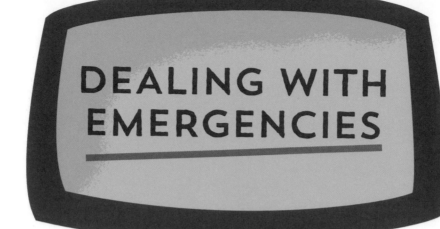

DEALING WITH EMERGENCIES

Astronauts have to be able to deal with emergencies.

LEARN HOW TO CHECK THE CONTROL PANEL AND TAKE ACTION

1. Check the temperature, oxygen (O_2) and carbon dioxide (CO_2) levels.
   If the arrow is in the green area, everything is as it should be.

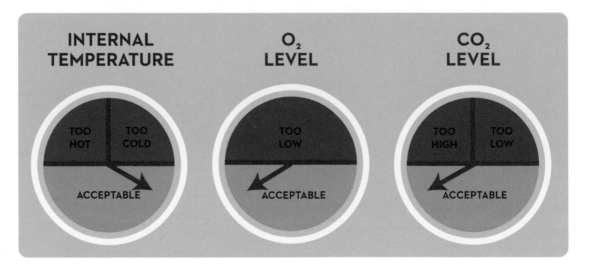

INTERNAL TEMPERATURE

TOO HOT | TOO COLD

ACCEPTABLE

O_2 LEVEL

TOO LOW

ACCEPTABLE

CO_2 LEVEL

TOO HIGH | TOO LOW

ACCEPTABLE

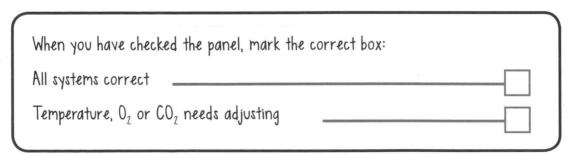

When you have checked the panel, mark the correct box:

All systems correct ⬜

Temperature, O_2 or CO_2 needs adjusting ⬜

2. Check the power systems. They should all be above the minimum power level.

POWER SYSTEMS

SOLAR CELLS   FUEL CELLS   BATTERIES

Minimum Power Level

When you have checked the panel, mark the correct box:

All power systems correct ☐

One or more power systems is below minimum level ☐

3. What action should you take to fix the problem?
Mark the correct action on the checklist below.

POWER SYSTEMS CHECKLIST

PROBLEM	SOLUTION	COMPLETED
Solar cells	Move solar panels	
Fuel cells	Switch on backup cells	
Batteries	Replace batteries	

Check your answers at the bottom of the page and then place your Mission Complete sticker here.

PLACE STICKER HERE

MISSION COMPLETE

Answers: The temperature, O₂ and CO₂ levels are OK. The fuel cells are below minimum so the backup cells need to be switched on.

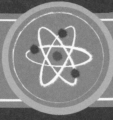

BUILD A ROCKET

The best way to find out how rockets work is to make one! By making a balloon rocket, you'll see how rockets move forward using propulsion.

MAKE YOUR OWN ROCKET

You will need:

a straw   a balloon   adhesive tape   about 13 feet of string

1. Push the string through the straw.

2. Tie each end of the string to the back of a chair and move the chairs apart so that the string is tight.

3. Blow up the balloon, but do not tie it. Pinch the end so the air does not escape.

4. Tape the balloon to the straw. You might need someone to hold the balloon while you do this.

5. Pull the balloon rocket to one end of the string, let go and watch as it is propelled.

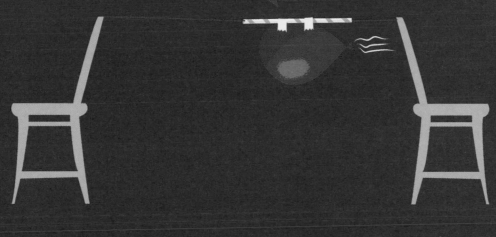

As the air rushes out of the balloon, it forces the balloon to move forward.

HOW ROCKETS WORK

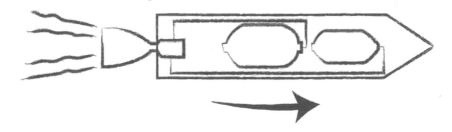

In a full-size rocket, fuel is burned to create a gas that rushes out of the back of the rocket, forcing it forward in exactly the same way as your balloon.

When you have launched your rocket, place your Mission Complete sticker here.

PLACE STICKER HERE

★ MISSION COMPLETE ★

—ORBITS—

A satellite is any object that orbits Earth. The Moon circles Earth and is a natural satellite, but there are also thousands of human-made satellites. Some are used for weather forecasting, some for communications. Others take photographs in space.

Satellites need power to launch them into space, but once they are there, they do not need any power to keep them orbiting Earth. This is because there is no air resistance to slow them down.

THERE ARE TWO REASONS SATELLITES STAY IN ORBIT:

1. The first is the pull of Earth's gravity. Gravity is a force that makes things fall to Earth. It keeps the satellite from heading off into space.

2. The second is the speed of the satellite, which keeps it from falling back to Earth.

Many satellites are **a few hundred miles** above Earth and circle it every **90 minutes**. However, the higher the orbit, the slower the satellites need to travel. At **22,000 miles** above Earth, satellites circle Earth **once a day**. This means they are always at the same spot above Earth (as long as they travel in the same direction) because Earth spins once a day.

UNDERSTAND HOW ORBITS WORK

You will need: an object that is securely fastened to a piece of string (a yo-yo is perfect).

1. Spin the object around and around in front of you.

2. Imagine that the string is the force of gravity, constantly pulling the object back to the center.

The speed of the object is what keeps the object from falling. This is how the two forces work together to keep satellites in space.

THE PLANET WITH TWO MOONS

Did you know that there are actually two moons in orbit around Mars?

The larger one is called **Phobos**, which means "fear" in Greek and the smaller one is called **Deimos**, which means "panic." They have very different orbits, with Phobos moving at an average of just under **6,000 miles** from Mars, while Deimos orbits at an average of nearly **15,000 miles**.

When you have completed the experiment, place your Mission Complete sticker here.

PLACE STICKER HERE

MISSION COMPLETE

— MARS —

On Mars the temperature varies from 86°F to -284°F. The average temperature is about -81°F—colder than the North Pole in winter.

There is very little atmosphere on Mars, which means astronauts would be exposed to the Sun's radiation.

Mars is known as the **Red Planet** because its rocks and soil are full of iron. The iron has turned into iron oxide, the scientific name for rust.

The planet is very dry, but scientists think that there was once water on Mars.

Mars' atmosphere is **95% carbon dioxide.** This is a poisonous gas, making it dangerous for astronauts.

Because Mars tilts, it has different seasons, causing weather changes at different times of the year. Winds create huge dust storms. If one blew up during an exploration, it would be impossible for astronauts to see where they were going.

Tests of Martian soil were carried out by the unmanned **Viking Explorer**. These showed no signs of life. Extreme temperatures, lack of water and oxygen, radiation and dust storms would make life on Mars very difficult.

Mars' gravity is about one third as strong as Earth's. Spacecraft would still need huge amounts of fuel to escape this gravity and blast off from the surface. Astronauts would need to leave their spacecraft in orbit and land in a smaller craft.

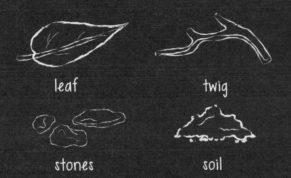

leaf

twig

stones

soil

Astronauts traveling to Mars will collect samples of rock and dust from the surface and underground.

PRACTICE SCIENTIFIC EXPLORATION SKILLS

Investigate your yard or a park to collect samples. You might include soil, different stones, a twig, a leaf and so on. If you are planning a trip to the beach, you might collect different shells and try to identify the creatures that lived in them. Draw them here.

When you have collected your samples, place the Mission Complete sticker here.

PLACE STICKER HERE

★ MISSION COMPLETE ★

INVESTIGATING
— GRAVITY —

If you jump up, you don't keep on rising but return quickly to Earth. This is because there is a force that keeps you and everything else on the ground. This force is called gravity. Gravity pulls all objects toward each other and is stronger for bigger objects. You never notice the pull from nearby objects, even from large buildings.

There is only one object large enough for you to feel the pull of gravity, and this is the planet you live on. The force of the gravity pulling you to Earth is your weight. Gravity is stronger for bigger objects, so your weight will vary on different planets because they are different sizes.

CALCULATE YOUR WEIGHT ON DIFFERENT PLANETS AND ON THE MOON

You will need: a bathroom scale and a calculator

1. Weigh yourself and write your weight in the space for planet Earth below.

2. Multiply your weight by the number shown to discover how much you would weigh on:

EARTH	THE MOON*	MARS*	JUPITER*
			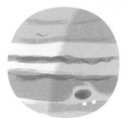

My weight on Earth is _____ lbs

My weight x 0.17 _____ lbs

My weight x 0.38 _____ lbs

My weight x 2.34 _____ lbs

*the planets and Moon are not shown in scale to Earth

PLACE STICKER HERE

When you have successfully figured out the different weights, place your Mission Complete sticker here.

Congratulations! You are now a...

—QUALIFIED—
MISSION SPECIALIST

NAME: Bobby Joe

The above named astronaut
is qualified to be a

MISSION SPECIALIST

and to take part in the first manned
mission to Mars.

Astronaut Academy would like
to wish you every success in your
historic mission.

GOOD LUCK!

QUALIFICATION DATE: Now

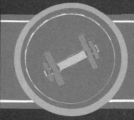

SPACE SUIT TRAINING

An astronaut has to move around and carry out tasks while wearing a space suit. This is not easy as there is a lot of equipment to carry, such as the large oxygen tanks on an astronaut's back.

COMPLETE AN OBSTACLE COURSE

You will need: a backpack, bulky but light objects (such as empty cereal boxes and empty plastic bottles), a stopwatch or a watch with a second hand

1. Load your backpack with the objects. Remember that this is not a weight-lifting exercise, so you must not have a heavy pack.

2. Put the backpack on and practice maneuvering through the course without losing your balance or bumping the backpack too much.

3. Do the course three times and ask a friend to record how quickly you can do it. See if you can get faster with practice.

SAFETY FIRST!
CHECK THE
PACK WEIGHT AND THE
COURSE WITH AN
ADULT BEFORE
YOU TRY IT.

Here are some ideas for your obstacle course:

Crawling under a rope

Heel-to-toe walking along a line

Jumping over a broom or stick

Jumping to touch something high

Hopscotch

Balancing along a plank

Crawling through a large, open cardboard box

Slalom

Record your times here in seconds:

Obstacle Course Times		
1st Run	2nd Run	3rd Run
_ _ _ _ _ _ _ _ seconds	_ _ _ _ _ _ _ seconds	_ _ _ _ _ _ _ seconds

When you have finished the course, place your Mission Complete sticker here.

PLACE STICKER HERE

★ MISSION COMPLETE ★

STAYING STRONG
—IN SPACE—

Every time we stand up, walk, or do anything, we use our muscles. This keeps them strong. However, in the weightlessness of space, muscles do not get exercise and start to waste away. In the time it would take to travel to Mars, you would become so weak that just walking around in a space suit would exhaust you.

To keep muscles strong, astronauts need to exercise. On the International Space Station, they exercise for at least two hours every day.

COMPLETE A SET OF EXERCISES DESIGNED FOR ASTRONAUTS

Do this routine on three different days and check them off on the chart when you have completed them.

Star Jumps
1. Crouch down bending your legs at the knees.
2. Jump up and make a star shape with your arms and legs.
3. Land with your feet together.
4. Repeat five times.

Squat Thrusts
1. Put your hands on the floor, shoulder width apart, and stretch your legs behind you.
2. Jump your legs forward so they are tucked underneath you.
3. Return to the first position.
4. Repeat five times.

Step Ups

1. Stand in front of the bottom step of the stairs.
2. Put your left foot on the step.
3. Put your right foot on the step.
4. Bring your left foot back to the floor.
5. Bring your right foot back to the floor.
6. Repeat five times.

Standing Squats

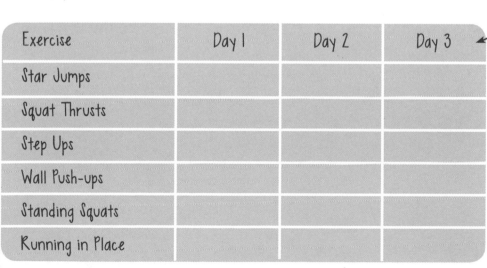

1. Stand with your feet shoulder width apart
2. Lower your body so your knees are bent.
3. Stand up.
4. Repeat five times.

Wall Push-ups

1. Stand facing a wall with feet shoulder width apart. Put your hands flat against the wall with arms stretched in front.
2. Slowly bend your arms until you are 2 inches from the wall. Keep your back straight.
3. Push away from the wall.
4. Repeat five times.

Running in Place

Run in place (without moving forward) for two minutes.

Put a check next to each exercise once you have completed it.

When you have completed the exercises, place your Mission Complete sticker here.

Exercise	Day 1	Day 2	Day 3
Star Jumps			
Squat Thrusts			
Step Ups			
Wall Push-ups			
Standing Squats			
Running in Place			

PLACE STICKER HERE

MISSION COMPLETE

WEIGHTLESSNESS — TRAINING —

Living in space is a real challenge! Astronauts go on space walks, perform repairs and do other jobs in a weightless environment. To practice, they use the nearest thing we have to space on Earth . . . water!

NASA's Neutral Buoyancy Laboratory in Houston, TX, is an enormous swimming pool 202 feet long, 102 feet wide and 40 feet deep. It is the world's largest indoor swimming pool and holds as much water as 11 Olympic-size pools.

There are full-size models of parts of the International Space Station underwater and astronauts spend hours working on these while wearing space suits.

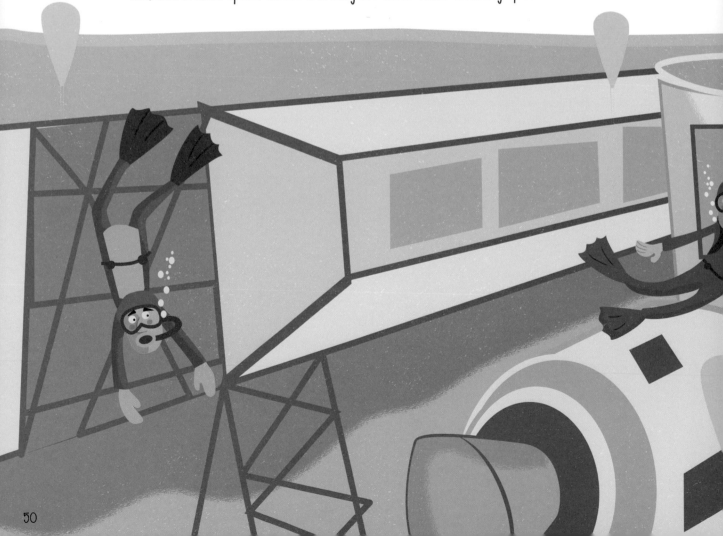

PRACTICE WEIGHTLESSNESS

You will need: dive toys, a parent or responsible adult

1. Throw a dive toy into the pool.

2. Dive underwater, collect the dive toy and bring it to the surface.

3. Once you can do this, try collecting two dive toys, then three, to practice moving around in a weightless environment.

You might even ask a friend to throw the dive toy into the pool while you have your back turned. Then, you will have to hunt for it!

When you have completed the challenge, place your Mission Complete sticker here.

PLACE STICKER HERE

MISSION COMPLETE

OUTDOOR FITNESS

Payload specialists need to be fit enough to cope with the demands of living in space. Agility and balance are also important.

You will need: markers such as sticks, chalk or a hula-hoop, a stopwatch, a tennis ball

EXERCISE 1 - FITNESS

Running is excellent for fitness. Start with a distance of 300 to 400 yards. Ask a friend to time you and record your lap times on the chart below. Complete this exercise three times.

Run 1	Run 2	Run 3
_____ mins	_____ mins	_____ mins

EXERCISE 2 - FITNESS

Interval training is another good way to build fitness. Jog while counting to 25. Then, sprint while you count to 10. Jog for another count of 25 and then sprint for 10. Repeat this until you have done four sprints. Check one of the boxes below every time you complete this.

Run 1	Run 2	Run 3

EXERCISE 3 - FITNESS AND AGILITY

This time you will practice running as fast as you can while moving through a row of markers. You can use anything you want for the markers, such as sticks or stones on the ground. The markers should be about five paces apart.

From the starting point, run through the markers as shown in the diagram. Ask a friend to time how long it takes you to complete three laps.

Run 1	Run 2	Run 3
_____ mins	_____ mins	_____ mins

EXERCISE 4 - BALANCE

Using chalk, draw a circle on the ground about 3 feet across. If you have a hula-hoop, use it for the circle instead. Walk ten paces away. Standing on one leg, try to throw a tennis ball into the target area. Complete this exercise ten times.

1	
2	
3	
4	
5	
6	
7	
8	
9	
10	

PLACE STICKER HERE

MISSION COMPLETE

When you have completed all the exercises, you have earned your Mission Complete sticker.

DESIGN YOUR MISSION PATCH

Astronauts wear different patches for different space missions. They work with artists to make sure each patch looks good and shows what the mission is about. When the patch design is finished, the astronauts proudly wear it on their space suits.

The most famous patch of all was made for the Apollo 11 Lunar Mission. It shows an American eagle landing on the Moon, with Earth in space behind it.

CREATE A PATCH FOR THE FIRST HUMAN MISSION TO MARS

On this page are examples of items you could include in your patch. Remember to include your name and the name of your mission in your patch.

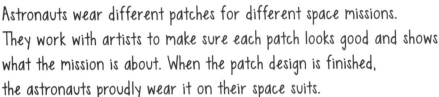

When you have designed and colored your patch,
place your Mission Complete sticker here.

PLACE
STICKER
HERE

★ MISSION COMPLETE ★

SPACE EXPLORATION
— TIMELINE —

The exciting thing about becoming an astronaut is that although a lot of exploration has already taken place, there is still a whole universe to explore!

THE TIMELINE BELOW SHOWS SOME OF THE KEY EVENTS THAT HAVE TAKEN PLACE IN SPACE EXPLORATION.

1957 Russia launches Sputnik 1, the first satellite

Also in **1957...**
The first dog in Earth orbit, Laika, was in Sputnik 2

1961 The Russian astronaut, Yuri Gagarin, becomes the first man in space

1963 Valentina Tereshkova is the first woman in space

1965 Aleksei Leonov makes the first ever space walk

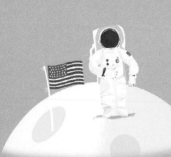

1969 Neil Armstrong is the first person to walk on the Moon

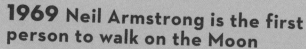

1971 The first space station, Salyut 1, is launched by Russia

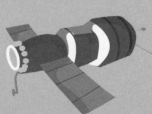

1976 The unmanned Viking 1 spacecraft lands on Mars

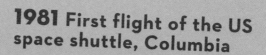

1981 First flight of the US space shuttle, Columbia

1990 Launch of the Hubble Space Telescope

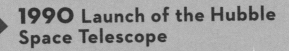

1995 The first time an American space shuttle docks with a space station (the Russian Mir station)

2000 Astronauts start living on the International Space Station

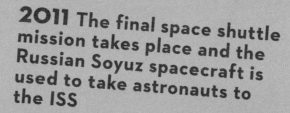

2011 The final space shuttle mission takes place and the Russian Soyuz spacecraft is used to take astronauts to the ISS

2013 NASA launch their first Orion rocket, designed to go to Mars one day

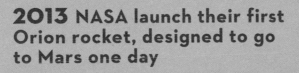

SPACE INFO

SPACE ROVERS

NASA created **lunar rovers** to enable astronauts to travel on the Moon. These vehicles were very lightweight but strong enough to cope with the Moon's rough surface and extreme temperatures.

The battery-powered rovers had a range of **88 miles** and a top speed of **6 mph**—about twice as fast as walking. They could carry two astronauts and their equipment, as well as the rock samples they collected.

There are now unmanned rovers on Mars. They have cameras and scientific equipment and are used to investigate conditions on the planet.

The Curiosity Rover only travels about **656 feet** per day as it takes a long time to respond to commands and because it needs to drive carefully over the rough surface. It also has tasks to carry out along the way, such as using its robot arm to scoop up samples of rock and soil.

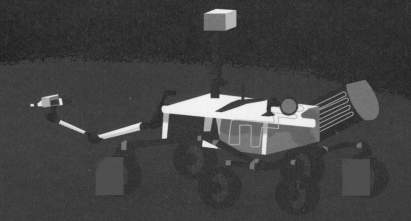

DESIGN A MARS BUGGY TO HELP YOU EXPLORE THE PLANET

You will need:

seats   storage   steering   scientific equipment   communication devices   cameras   tools

Remember that the surface of Mars has difficult terrain to navigate so make sure your buggy is able to handle it. Draw your picture below.

When you have drawn your space buggy, stick your Mission Complete sticker here.

PLACE STICKER HERE

MISSION COMPLETE

MISSION TO MARS!

Astronauts will have to overcome many challenges to reach Mars, such as growing their own food and exercising regularly to prevent muscles from wasting away.

TEST YOUR SKILLS BY SOLVING THESE THREE CHALLENGES
Each problem has only one correct answer. Since you have worked through the book, you should be able to find the right one.

PROBLEM 1

Traveling to Mars and spending time on the surface will expose astronauts to high levels of radiation, which can cause illnesses. This problem can be overcome by:

A Making sure the astronauts are healthy before they leave.

B Using special materials in the spacecraft and space suits to shield against radiation.

C Sending a doctor into space with the astronauts.

D Giving the astronauts a medical checkup when they return.

Mars has gravity, though not as much as Earth. The return trip will need to escape Mars' gravity in order for the spacecraft to lift off. This problem can be overcome by:

A Leaving the spacecraft orbiting Mars and sending down a smaller, lighter

There are countless rocks flying through space. Even small ones can cause massive amounts of damage since they can travel at thousands of miles per hour. This problem can be overcome by:

A Training astronaut pilots to dodge meteors

B Making sure the spacecraft travels faster than the meteors.

C Putting weapons on the spacecraft to shoot down meteors.

D Developing strong space suits for astronauts and armor for the spacecraft.

Check your answers at the bottom of the page and place your Mission Complete sticker here if you got them all correct.

PLACE STICKER HERE

★ MISSION COMPLETE ★

Answers: 1=B, 2=A, 3=D

Congratulations! You are now a...

— QUALIFIED —
PAYLOAD SPECIALIST

NAME: *Billy Joe*

The above named astronaut is
qualified to be a

PAYLOAD SPECIALIST

and to take part in the first
manned mission to Mars.

Astronaut Academy would like to wish
you every success in your historic mission.

GOOD LUCK!

QUALIFICATION DATE: 1/2/2500

WELL DONE!

You have successfully completed all your tasks
and finished your space cadet training.

You are now ready to graduate from the Astronaut Academy.

dangerous job. I promise to continue to develop my skills and complete
my work to the best of my ability.

2. All space missions depend upon the astronaut
team. I will always put the interests of the
team and the mission first.

Draw a picture or
glue a photo of
your face here.

3. I will always be honest and respectful with my
fellow astronauts and with members of the public.

4. I will not behave in any way that puts
members of my team or anyone else at risk.

5. I will support all astronauts in their work
and in keeping the Astronaut's Code.

Signed:
- -

SPACE GOODIES!

IN THIS SECTION YOU WILL FIND LOTS OF SPACE GOODIES TO PLAY WITH:

- A pull-out space exploration timeline poster
- A Mission to Mars board game
- Lots of fun space stickers
- A spacecraft model (on the flaps of the book)

MISSION TO MARS GAME INSTRUCTIONS

You'll find this game board on the reverse side of the pull-out poster. There are press-out game cards, playing counters and a dice in this section too.

MISSION TO MARS

You are in a race to be the first person to land on Mars. Launching from Earth, roll the dice to see how many spaces to move your rocket. If you land on a red rocket, pick up a Mission to Mars card and follow the instructions. The first player to reach Mars is the winner!

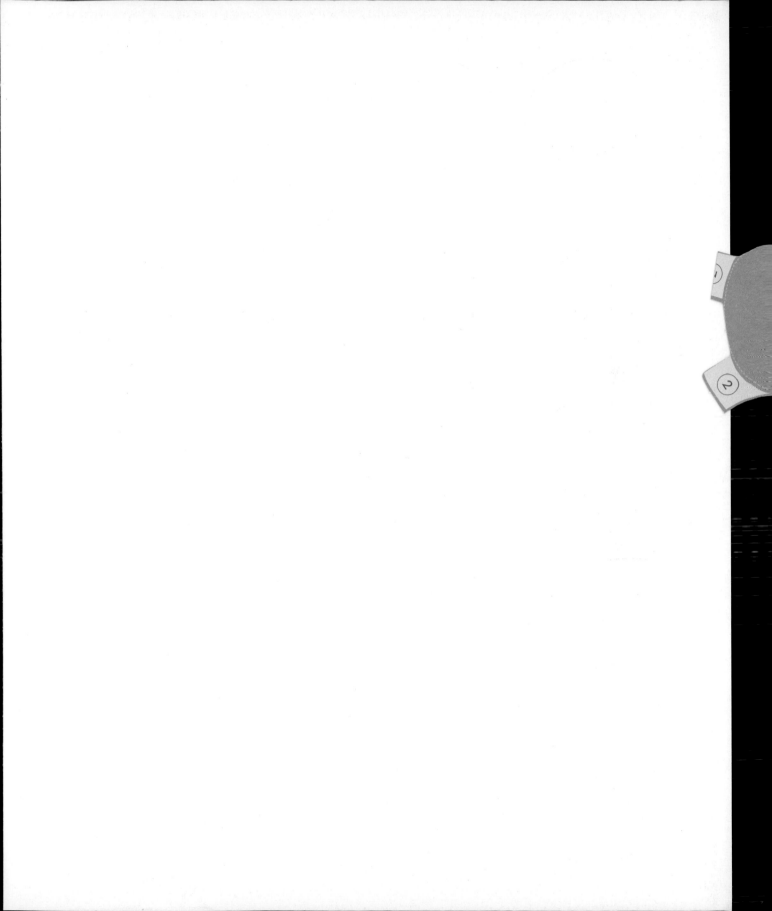

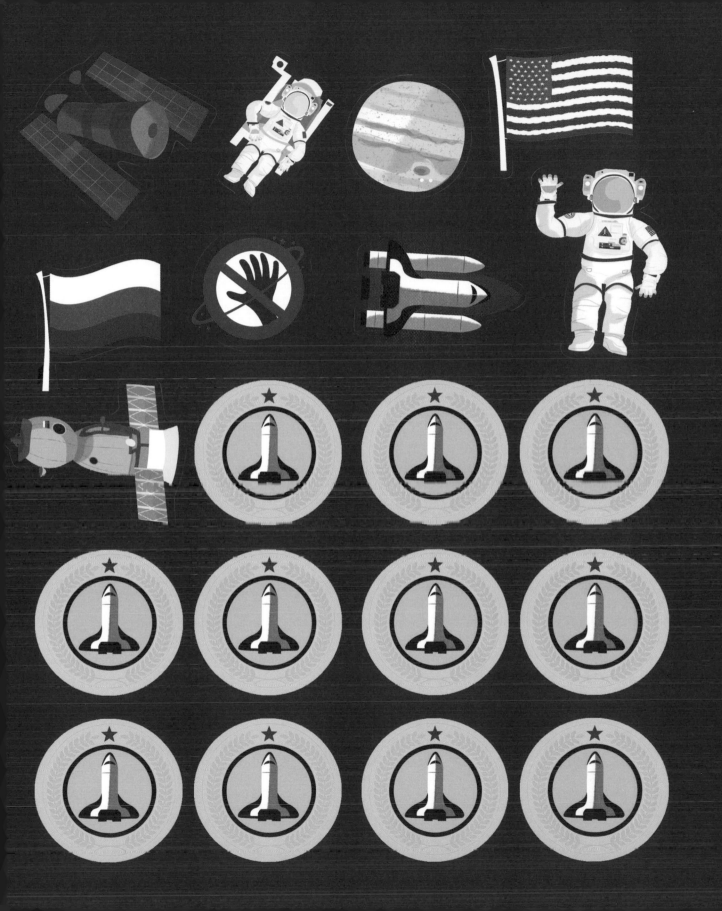

MISSION TO MARS CARDS

YOUR FITNESS REGIME SHOWS YOU HAVE KEPT MOST OF YOUR MUSCLE STRENGTH DURING THE JOURNEY

MOVE FORWARD 2 SPACES

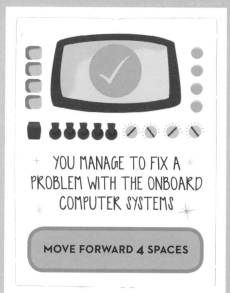

YOU MANAGE TO FIX A PROBLEM WITH THE ONBOARD COMPUTER SYSTEMS

MOVE FORWARD 4 SPACES

YOU HAVE SUCCESSFULLY GROWN YOUR FIRST CROP OF SPACE FOOD

MOVE FORWARD 6 SPACES

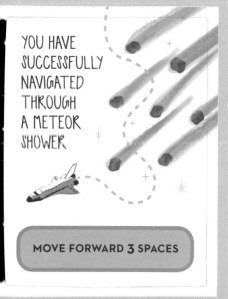

YOU HAVE SUCCESSFULLY NAVIGATED THROUGH A METEOR SHOWER

MOVE FORWARD 3 SPACES

YOU RECEIVE MESSAGES FROM YOUR FAMILY WHEN THEY VISIT MISSION CONTROL

MOVE FORWARD 1 SPACE

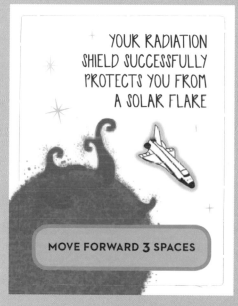

YOUR RADIATION SHIELD SUCCESSFULLY PROTECTS YOU FROM A SOLAR FLARE

MOVE FORWARD 3 SPACES

GAME COUNTERS

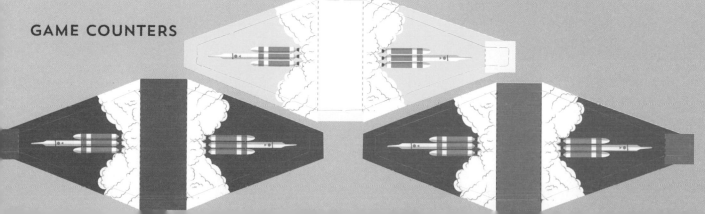

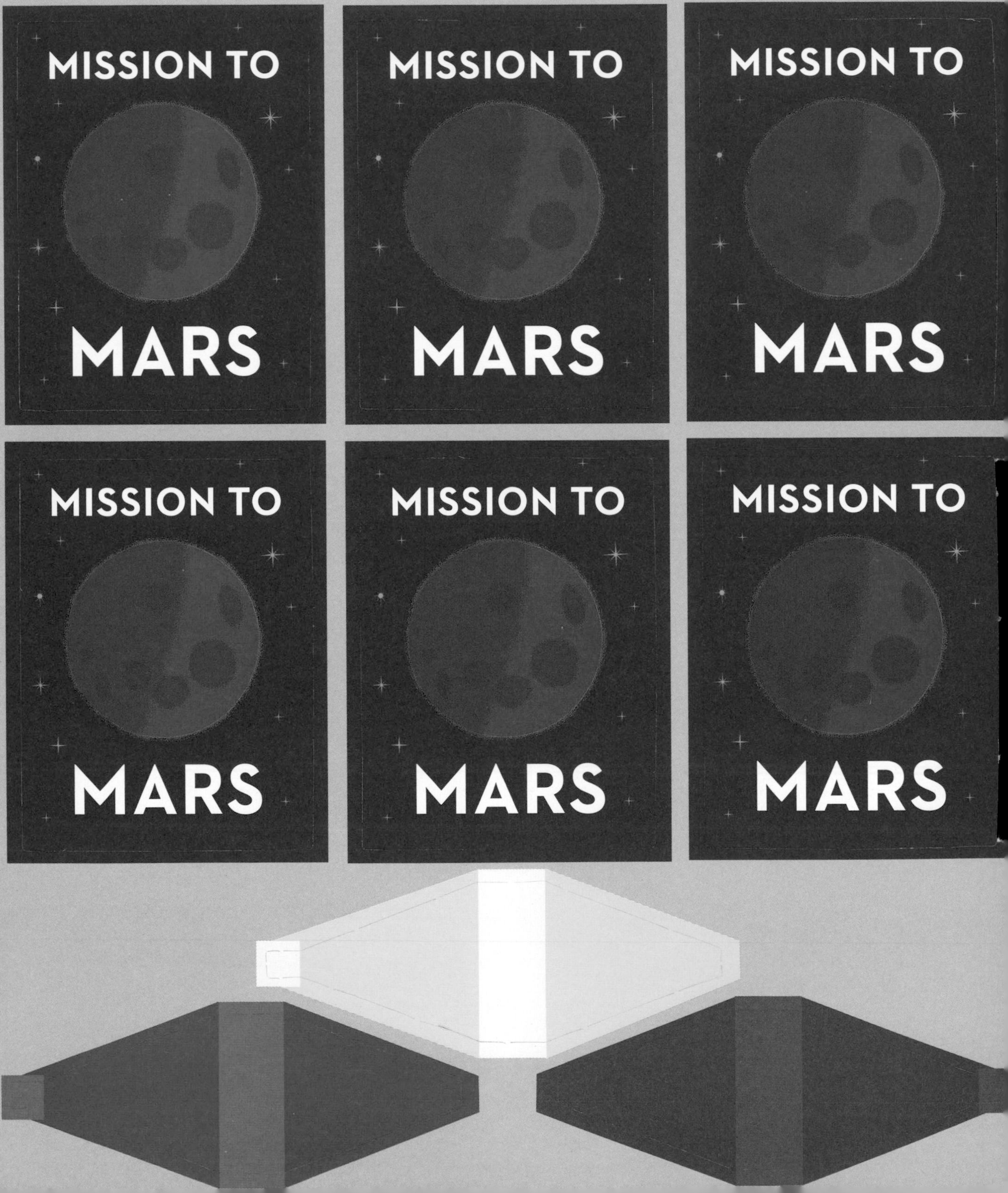
MISSION TO
MARS
MISSION TO
MARS
MISSION TO
MARS
MISSION TO
MARS
MISSION TO
MARS
MISSION TO
MARS

MISSION TO MARS CARDS

ONE OF YOUR CREW IS ILL

MOVE BACK 3 SPACES

YOU HAVE LOST COMMUNICATION WITH MISSION CONTROL

MOVE BACK 4 SPACES

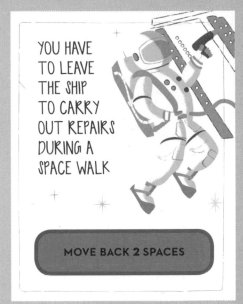

YOU HAVE TO LEAVE THE SHIP TO CARRY OUT REPAIRS DURING A SPACE WALK

MOVE BACK 2 SPACES

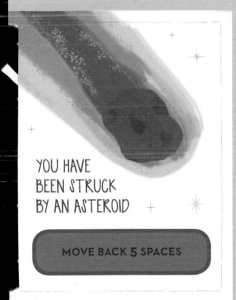

YOU HAVE BEEN STRUCK BY AN ASTEROID

MOVE BACK 5 SPACES

YOU ARE FEELING HOMESICK AFTER SO LONG IN SPACE

MOVE BACK 1 SPACE

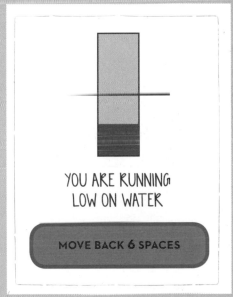

YOU ARE RUNNING LOW ON WATER

MOVE BACK 6 SPACES

DICE

GAME COUNTER

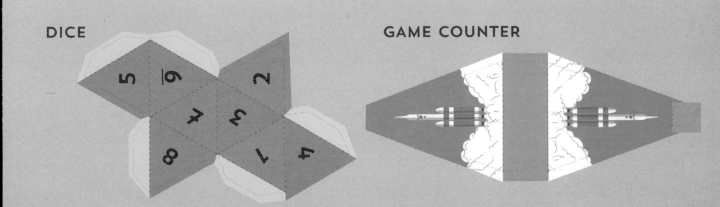

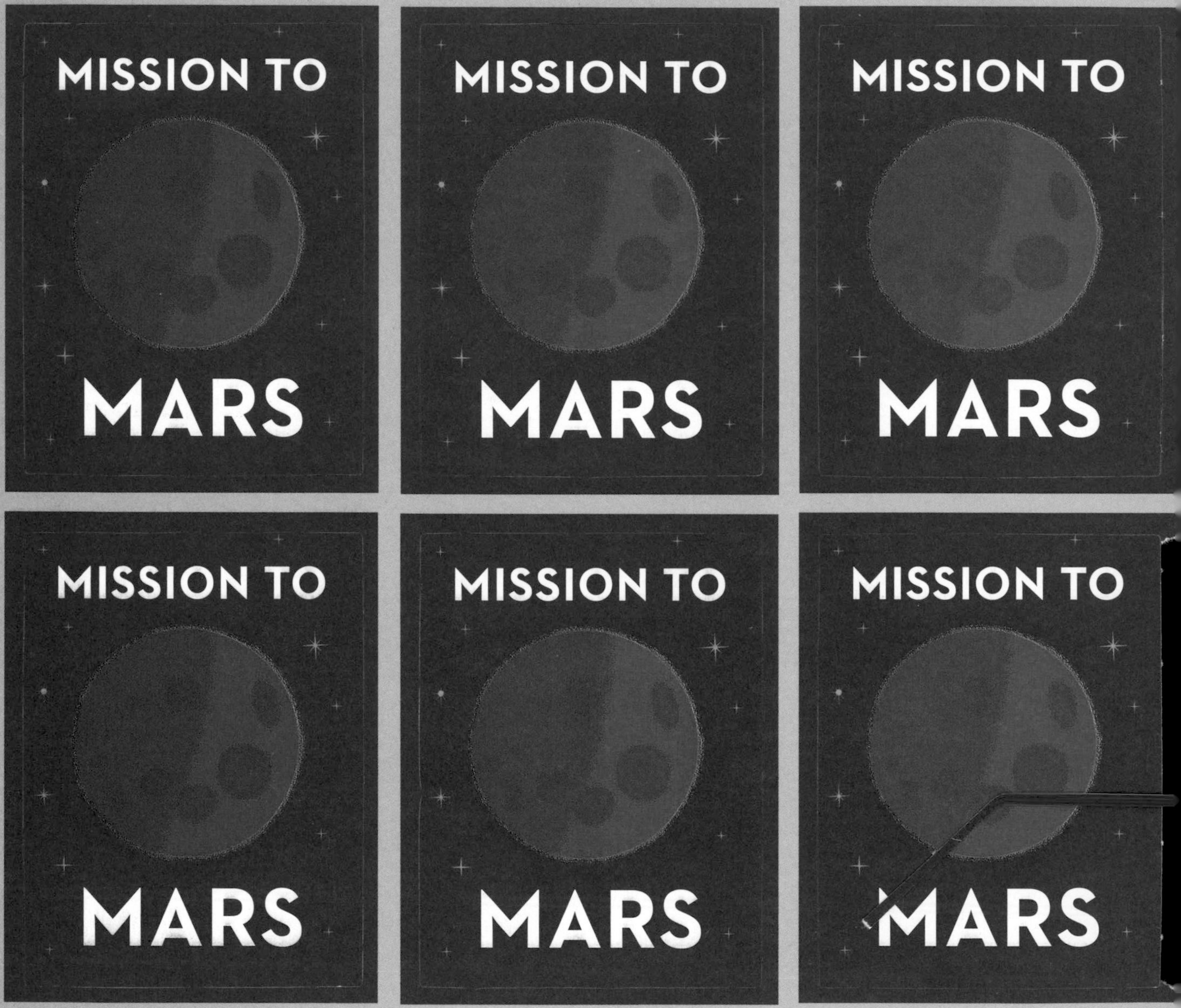

MISSION TO

MARS

MISSION TO

MARS

MISSION TO

MARS

MISSION TO

MARS

MISSION TO

MARS

MISSION TO

MARS